Su

or

Sour Grapes

By Brad Harford

WinePress Publications

Published by
WinePress Publications
7946 W. Bopp Road
Tucson, AZ 85735

ISBN: **0-9650947-0-7**

Contents

Acknowledgments

Reba Harford, my wife, who experienced most of the things in this book with me. She inspired me throughout the process of writing and publishing.

Bud & Helen Harford, my father and mother, who supported me emotionally and financially in this effort. This book is in memory of my mother who is now in heaven. She read the first draft of this work before she passed away.

Kelly St John a daughter and friend who drew the artwork for the cover design.

And to my friends, new and old, who encouraged me, contributed ideas and critiqued the work as it developed.

Thank you all.

Introduction

This is a "How-to" book written for the average person. It is a book about life. Is it possible to have a life that is enjoyable and rewarding? You may be surviving but not enjoying your life. This book outlines some simple principles that can bring positive change in *your* life. Pressure comes in many forms and we cannot live and grow without it. We all experience it in some form but we all react differently.

Our lifestyle is the fruit of who we are, what we know and how we think. As we encounter the pressures of daily life, one of two things is squeezed out of us in some measure; ***Sweet Wine or Sour Grapes***. Sweet wine makes lives merry and brings medicinal, healing value. Sour grapes irritate, aggravate and leave a bad taste in your mouth. Most people do fine when things are going OK and there is no apparent pressure, but facing pressure reveals what we are really made of. The goal of this book is to help us be sweet wine rather than sour grapes when we are squeezed.

This is not a clinical or highly technical book. It is written in plain language using common examples and illustrations. Most of us make decisions and communicate based on our perception. We will discuss how perception, whether accurate or in-accurate can change our lives.

*Perception, whether right or wrong,
Is reality to the perceiver.*

Regardless of your current status, there is something in this book that can enhance your life in some way.

The information in this book has been proven by the practice and experience of many thousands of people over many generations. It has worked in the past and is still working effectively today. Once again, this is not a clinical book, it is a practical book. It is intended for those of normal physical and mental health. For clinical problems we recommend seeing the appropriate professional.

The source material for most of this book is the Holy Bible and the experience of many ordinary people. Although the bible is the source material, this is not a religious book. It is a practical application guide. Unless otherwise designated, bible references are taken from the New King James Version.

May your journey through this book be a pleasant and profitable one.

Questions or comments about this book may be directed to the publisher.

Chapter 1

Principles of Life

I will begin by sharing a brief story of my own life. In October 1991 I was told that due to a reduction in the work-force at the company I worked for, my position was being terminated. I had begun employment with this company 19 years earlier, not long after completing a term in the Air Force. Most of my adult life had been spent working for this company. This situation had great potential for causing stress. The following chapters contain the principles that I applied in my life during this time of change and uncertainty. I believe that it can be helpful to you also. More details of my unemployment and the subsequent years are described in later chapters.

A partial definition of STRESS is: (*pressure, strain or tension.*) The emotional and mental strain and pressure on individuals seems to be continually increasing in the 90's. Most of the news that we hear seems to be discouraging rather than encouraging. How can a person have peace of mind, security and tranquility in a time of such turmoil? The answer is simple, but by no means easy.

1

> # Two people can face the same situation and one suffer from stress while the other is at peace

We will always encounter pressure in our lives. Without pressure or resistance we could not grow. Without challenges we would become stagnant. The difference between pressure that causes growth, and (STRESS), that can cause premature age, sickness or even death, is the way we process them in our mind. What we know and how we think can make the difference between peace or anxiety in any given situation. Two people can face the same situation and one suffer from stress while the other is at peace. The difference is in what they know and who they know. Following are several principles that are shared and repeated frequently throughout this book.

1. Things we **think** develop into action and lifestyle.

2. **Faith**, (trusting belief), precedes reality.

3. **Truth** supersedes fact that is discerned through our five senses.

4. Knowledge of truth brings power.

5. Things we believe and words we **speak**, dramatically effect our lives.

6. We **reap** what we have been **sowing**.

These principles will be explained in detail and examples showing how to apply them to life's situations will be given. Many of the things we discuss will sound familiar to those who have studied psychology or read self-help books but we will be taking a different approach.

Man was created as a threefold being, (spirit, soul and body). The spirit is the life force of a person, the deep inner being where things beyond or outside the natural realm are processed. The Soul, which comes from the greek word "psuche", is (*the mind, the will and the emotions*). Our senses are related to the soul. The body is the physical house that the spirit and soul live in. Psychology deals with the principles that relate to the soul. The term psychology is essentially; psuche or psyche-ology, or, (the study of the soul). We will also be dealing with the spirit and it's relationship to the soul.

As we think about something and rehearse it in our minds, it affects our ability to perform what we are thinking about. This is an example of the principle that thoughts develop into action. Consider a simple basketball illustration.

An experiment was conducted using three groups. All three groups participated in a session of shooting baskets. The scores were recorded. A second session was scheduled for a later date. Group one was not to practice until the next session. Group two was to practice several times before the next session and group three was to perform only mental practice before the next session. Group three was to go through all the motions of shooting baskets in their minds without physically touching a basketball. The result at the next session was as follows: Group one showed no improvement and groups two and three showed about the same level of improvement. This demonstrates the transforming power of the mind and it's thinking processes. You may ask; what does this have to do with overcoming stress? In the next section we will discuss the mind and the thinking process and how it affects our lives.

Simply thinking differently can reduce stress.

Before we go on let's lay a foundation to build on. The bible is the resource material for most of the information in this book. Since God created us and the world that we live in, it makes sense to use His handbook to learn how to deal with life. We will be discussing laws and principles, not religion. Religion in most cases sucks the life out of a person and doesn't put anything back in. This causes stress and we are looking for a cure, not another cause. This may appear to be a contradictory statement but it is explained and a definition of religion is also given in a later chapter. The bible contains the principles of life and the truth that can make us free. Read on and judge for yourself. We will be looking at the nuts and bolts of life from God's viewpoint.

Chapter 2

THOUGHTS LEAD TO ACTION: Principle #1

Doctors have told us that more than three fourths of physical ailments originate in the mind (psychosomatic). While researching material for a report on placebos, I read some amazing accounts of how our bodies will change as a result of a change in our thinking. People have recovered completely from disease and ailments ranging from minor to life threatening, after taking a placebo. What this means is that people were given doses of inert substances while THINKING that they were receiving medicine that would cure them. The results were that these people were cured. The process of being made well took place in and through their minds because they believed that they had received something that would cure them. This vividly illustrates the effect that our thinking has on our bodies.

The bible is God's point of view. It reveals what He is like and how He thinks. Many of the things we will draw out of the bible will sound like things that you have read in psychology literature. This is because the bible is a handbook for the whole person; spirit, soul and body. Psychology attempts to understand the soul of man therefore true psychology will agree with the bible concerning the soul. The following are some verses that emphasize the importance of our thinking in relationship to our lifestyle and circumstances.

Romans 12:2 And do not be conformed to this world, but be *[transformed by the renewing of your mind]*, that you may prove what is that good and acceptable and perfect will of God.

The bible says that we should be TRANSFORMED by the renewing or renovating of our minds. This transformation is like what happens when a caterpillar is transformed into a butterfly. If we change our thinking, our lives change. This change comes by a continual renewal of our thinking.

Philippians 4:8-9 Finally, brethren, whatever things are true, whatever things are noble, whatever things are just, whatever things are pure, whatever things are lovely, whatever things are of good report, if there is any virtue and if there is anything praiseworthy; *[meditate on these things]*. {9} The things which you learned and received and heard and saw in me, these do, and the God of peace will be with you.

Here we are shown what to focus our thoughts on, i.e. (Things that are true, just, pure, etc.). If we meditate and do God's word, He, the God of PEACE, will be with us.

Joshua 1:8   "This Book of the Law shall not depart from your mouth, but you shall *[meditate in it day and night]*, that you may observe to do according to all that is written in it. For then you will make your way prosperous, and then you will have good success.

Psalms 1:1-3   Blessed is the man who walks not in the counsel of the ungodly, Nor stands in the path of sinners, Nor sits in the seat of the scornful; {2} But his delight is in the law of the LORD, And *in His law he [meditates day and night]*. {3} He shall be like a tree Planted by the rivers of water, That brings forth its fruit in its season, Whose leaf also shall not wither; And whatever he does shall prosper.

Meditation simply means; (to turn something over in your mind or to talk to yourself about it). According to these verses if God's word and His principles are always on our mind, the resulting lifestyle will be success and prosperity. We will be fruitful. Look at Galatians 5:22 in your bible to see what fruit is. Love, Joy, Peace, etc. These things sound desirable if we are suffering from stress.

An occasional thought won't change our lives. Transforming power comes with consistent and disciplined thinking. The importance of what we think is revealed in the verses we just read. Changing your thinking can change your whole outlook on life without your environment changing at all.

When you think about life's problems, consider God as the master engineer that designed and created us. View the bible, (His word), as the operating manual and warranty aggreement for His creation which includes us. The scriptures we will be considering are principles that God's creation operates by. They are as accurate and dependable as the laws of physics are. If we apply them correctly they will give the declared results every time.

Chapter 3

THE CURE

Let's look at the remedy God has for us. It can turn pressure into a builder rather than a destroyer. It is the MEDICINE to relieve stress. We will talk about the application of the medicine a little later. God's word and His power are the medicine that will relieve stress and bring victory to our lives.

Jesus said we are His disciples, we will know the truth, and the truth will make us FREE, **(IF)** we abide in His word (John 8:31-32). God has a truth, a principle and a provision for every situation that we encounter. They are found in His word.

2 Timothy 3:16-17 All Scripture is given by inspiration of God, and is profitable for doctrine, for reproof, for correction, for instruction in righteousness, {17} that the man of God may be complete, thoroughly equipped for every good work.

The bible was given to us so that we would be completely equipped for life. It contains the answers, but we must know what they are in order to apply them. We learn what they are by abiding in His word. Abiding infers a continuous action, not once per week or month. This means reading the bible, as well as talking and listening to God on a regular basis.

Many bibles have a topical index that is helpful in finding references for specific subjects. This type of index could help you find the truth concerning your situation. Keep in mind that finding the medicine is only the first step in the process. Let's look at a few examples.

Fear and worry are common causes of stress. Anything that makes us FEEL powerless or helpless can cause stress. Notice I used the word FEEL. Most of the time when we worry, we are worrying for no legitimate reason. In other words our worry is based on feelings, which have no truth to support them. Fear of the unknown causes a great deal of worry. Following are a few biblical cures for stress causing conditions. These examples deal with various types of fear, worry and anxiety.

Philippians 4:6-7 Be anxious for nothing, but in everything by prayer and supplication, with thanksgiving, let your requests be made known to God; {7} and the *[peace of God]*, which surpasses all understanding, [will guard your hearts and minds] through Christ Jesus. (Be

11

anxious for nothing means don't worry about anything)

If we practice what verse 6 says, we will have our hearts and minds guarded by incomprehensible peace. The next verse tells us that Jesus has given us His peace.

John 14:27 "*Peace I leave with you*, My [peace I give to you]; not as the world gives do I give to you. [Let not your heart be troubled, neither let it be afraid].

The next three verses reveal that fear is not from God and that He does not want us to be overcome by it. We also see that Love drives out fear.

2 Timothy 1:7 For *God has not given us a spirit of fear*, but of [power and of love and of a sound mind].

Romans 8:15 For you *did not receive the spirit of bondage again to fear,* but [you received the Spirit of adoption] by whom we cry out, "Abba, Father."

1 John 4:18 There is no fear in love; but *[perfect love casts out fear]*, because fear involves torment. But he who fears has not been made perfect in love.

Fear of failing financially grips the hearts of many in today's society. The following truths can bring great comfort and security in this area.

Matthew 6:31-33 "Therefore do not worry, saying, 'What shall we eat?' or 'What shall we drink?' or 'What shall we wear?' {32} "For after all these things the Gentiles seek. For your heavenly Father knows that you need all these things. {33} ["But seek first the kingdom of God and His righteousness, and *all these things shall be added to you]*.

Philippians 4:19 And my [God shall *supply all your need]* according to His riches in glory by Christ Jesus.

Proverbs 3:9-10 Honor the LORD with your possessions, And with the firstfruits of all your increase; {10} *[So your barns will be filled with plenty]*, And your vats will overflow with new wine.

Malachi 3:10 Bring all the tithes into the storehouse, That there may be food in My house, And try Me now in this," Says the LORD of hosts, "If I will not open for you the windows of heaven

And *[pour out for you such blessing* That there will not be room enough to receive it].

These verses speak of money and material things. Remember, we are spirit, soul, and body. God has made provision for all three areas of our lives.

Health care is another area that is covered under God's plan. The next few verses speak of healing for our bodies and length of life.

Spiritual medicine is similar to natural medicine, if we don't apply it properly it could hurt rather than help

---

1 Peter 2:24   who Himself bore our sins in His own body on the tree, that we, having died to sins, might live for righteousness; by whose stripes *[you were healed]*.

Psalms 103:2-3   Bless the LORD, O my soul, And forget not all His benefits: {3} Who forgives all your iniquities, **[Who *heals all your diseases]*,**

Proverbs 3:1-2   My son, do not forget my law, But let your heart keep my commands; {2} For [length of days and *long life* And peace they will add to you].

Worrying about your health can make you sick.

The preceding scriptures have given us an example of God's medicine for fear and worry. There is a biblical provision for every problem or situation in our lives. It would be helpful to learn to use bible study aids that can help locate answers to specific problems when they arise. Some examples of these tools are: [*concordances, bible dictionaries and the previously mentioned topical indexes*]. These helps will assist in finding the truth. Once we have the truth, we have the medicine. Spiritual medicine is similar to natural medicine, if we don't apply it properly it could hurt rather than help. We must therefore learn to use it correctly.

Chapter 4

APPLICATION

It should be clear at this point that I am writing from a Christian perspective. As we talk about the application of these cures for stress and anxiety, it will become clear that without faith in God, there is not much hope for gaining **lasting** victory over stress. Victory simply means; (to defeat or drive out something). We are not seeking to sooth stress and anxiety but to beat it. Drugs (tranquilizers, etc.) are a temporary method of help that the traditional system uses. They don't defeat the problem they just delay and sooth it. In order to beat stress we must go beyond just the mind and body. Lasting victory, originates in the spirit.

It's easy enough to see that God's word is the solution for the causes of stress. Simply knowing the solution doesn't make it happen. Faith is involved in overcoming stress by acting on God's word concerning a situation. According to Hebrews 11:1, faith is the substance of things HOPED for and the evidence of things NOT SEEN. When we are stressed out, the thing that we hope for is peace. Faith that brings hope into reality is developed by continually hearing God's word. (See Romans 10:17) Faith involves the inner man (the spirit).

Most of our stress comes from the way we think

Remember that most of our stress comes from the way we think, therefore we must change the way we think. Changing our thinking is not like a one time pill or shot that brings eternal happiness. It must be a continuing lifestyle. The bible says that our observable lifestyle reflects the thoughts that are in our heart. **(Prov 23:7)** The (*thoughts of our heart*) are not passing thoughts, they are our frame of mind. God said that if we meditate in His word day and night we would prosper and have success. Everyone may have short periods of rest and peace in their life but being a peaceful person requires a lifestyle of peace. Now we are talking about SOWING AND REAPING. We will discuss this principle in a later chapter. Faith is illustrated in the sowing of a seed. Knowing that it has been planted and is being cared for brings confidence that something will sprout up. A farmer expects a crop in his field when he has planted, even though at the time there is no visible evidence of anything in the field. We should plant God's word in our heart and expect the promised result. The wise person is continually planting God's word in his heart. The result is a continual harvest of what has been planted. This is the key to victorious lifestyle; **continuous sowing** and **continuous reaping.**

Chapter 5

FAITH: Principle #2

As we read the remedies for stress, worry, etc. they are simple. It's the application that we often have problems with. Let's take a closer look at the operation of faith at this point. Memorizing every verse in the bible will not help you if you do not have faith. Faith is believing something and trusting in it from your heart, not just with your head. Following are a few verses that speak of faith, and then a story to illustrate it.

Hebrews 11:6   But without faith *it is impossible to please Him*, for he who comes to God must believe that He is, and that He is a rewarder of those who diligently seek Him.

It is clear that a person must have faith to please God. Every christian has been given a measure or portion of faith. Too often we think of faith as some force or thing that is nearly impossible to acquire. The truth is, God has given each of us a portion of faith and it is not difficult to maintain it and cause it to grow.

Romans 12:3   For I say, through the grace given to me, to everyone who is among you, not to think of himself more highly than he ought to think, but to think soberly, as [God has dealt to *each one a measure of faith]*.

Romans 10:17 So then *faith [comes by hearing]*, and hearing by the word of God.

Faith comes from and is strengthened by, a continuous hearing of God's word. You may have heard the phrase "you get what you pay for". Faith that brings change is costly, although the price is not money. Spending time reading and pondering the bible takes a great deal of discipline. Spending time talking to God and listening for His response also takes time and discipline. I know several people who have attained a black belt level in the martial arts. These people have a high level of proficiency in their style of martial art. The point is this; it took a great deal of discipline, practice, study and time for these people to attain their black belt level. Effective faith also takes that kind of diligence on our part. It is not a difficult thing but it is not automatic, we must work it out, we must practice it. If we wait till we have time to develop our faith, we will never do it. We must take time.

Hearing only with our ears, does not build faith. The (word of God) translated in Romans 10:17 is the greek word "rhema"; pronounced (ray-mah). The word rhema denotes a hearing that engages our spirit. The mind is involved but it goes deeper than simply the intellect. A person could have the whole bible memorized and not overcome stress or anything else if the information was in the head only, but not in the heart.

Following is an example that illustrates faith. It shows the difference between believing simply with the mind and believing with the heart.

Faith will cause us to get into the wheelbarrow

A man once did a performance at Niagara Falls. He had a tightrope strung across the space between the river banks. He walked back and forth on the rope. Then he wheeled a wheelbarrow across and back. The crowd was impressed. Next the man put a 200 pound bag of sand in the wheelbarrow and wheeled it across and back. Then the man asked the crowd if they believed that he could take a person across and back in his wheelbarrow. Of course they did believe and they said so. His next question was; "who would like to go first?". He had no volunteers.

The difference between believing in our mind (intellect only) and believing with our heart (faith), is that faith would allow us to get into the wheelbarrow while simply believing would not. You can also see that if faith was not present first, no action would be taken. This illustrates the fact that FAITH PRECEDES REALITY. The scripture reference for this is Hebrews 11:1.

Hebrews 11:1   Now faith is the substance of things hoped for, the evidence of things not seen.

In this verse, substance means a supporting structure or a foundation. Faith is the support of things that are hoped for. Evidence means the undeniable proof of something. Here, it is the proof of things that are not yet seen. This is why faith always precedes reality. Skepticism says, "I'll believe it if I can see it". Faith says, "if I believe it I will see it".

God has given us each a measure of faith. It is up to us to exercise it so that it will grow stronger.

Chapter 6

TRUTH: Principle #3

The next principle that we will address involves truth. We may have lots of faith, but if we don't know the truth it won't benefit much.

Our soul (mind, will, etc.) is a very significant part of our triune make-up but unless the spiritual portion of our life is addressed, we have not dealt with the whole person. People who have a relationship with God not only have the power of their minds but they also have the power of God and His word in their lives. Too many times this wonderful mind that God has given us becomes our greatest enemy. Because our mind has so much affect on our lives it is very important that we put truth into it. To overcome the negative affect of stress we must know the TRUTH. Truth is of SPIRITUAL origin. You may ask, what is truth? The bible presents truth in two ways as you can see in the following scriptures:

John 14:6 Jesus said to him, "I am the way, the *[truth]*, and the life. No one comes to the Father except through Me.

John 17:17 "Sanctify them by Your truth. Your word is *[truth]*.

John 8:32 "And you shall know the truth, and the *[truth]* shall make you free."

1. God is truth.
2. His word is truth.
3. Truth frees us, from stress or anything else.

Truth supersedes fact. Here is an illustration:

It is a **fact** that water will not stand up like a wall without being held in some type of a container. The **truth** is that God caused the waters of the Red Sea to stand up like a wall while the people of Israel traveled through them on dry land. (Exodus 14:22) It is a **fact** that if you throw a combustible item into a furnace it will burn up. The **truth** is that God protected three Hebrew men who were thrown into a furnace. The furnace was so hot that it killed the men who threw them into it, but they were not harmed. (See Daniel chapter 3)

The bible, God's word, is truth and we have seen in these examples that truth takes precedence over natural fact. Many times the truth of God may contradict what we see or hear with our five senses. You might think that these examples were special cases and God wouldn't do such things today.

Truth is absolute. It is always true regardless of what we think or feel

Let me share some scripture and related experiences. Try to think of what God is really like and not what you may have previously perceived. The bible says that He does not change, He is the same yesterday, today and forever. (See Malachi 3:6 & Hebrews 13:8) It also says that God is not partial (Acts 10:34 & Romans 2:11). What God has done for His people in the past, He will do again in the present if the need arises.

James 5:14-15 Is anyone among you sick? Let him call for the elders of the church, and let them pray over him, anointing him with oil in the name of the Lord. {15} And the prayer of faith will save the sick, and the Lord will raise him up. And if he has committed sins, he will be forgiven.

There are many places in scripture that show God's desire for His children to be well. James 5:14-15 is one example of many. I have heard testimonies of divine healing resulting from prayer from many people of varied backgrounds. The evidence supports the truth that God does what His word says He will.

My wife was diagnosed as having cysts in her body that were to be surgically removed. We prayed, believing that God would take care of her according to His word. When she went to the specialist that she had been referred to, the cysts were gone. God had healed her body without using natural means. We have seen people healed of terminal cancer. These are illustrations of truth altering the conditions in the physical environment. Another application is in the area of material needs.

Luke 6:38   "Give, and it will be given to you: good measure, pressed down, shaken together, and running over will be put into your bosom. For with the same measure that you use, it will be measured back to you."

Philippians 4:19   And my God shall supply all your need according to His riches in glory by Christ Jesus.

These two verses speak of giving, receiving and God meeting our needs. A friend of ours had an experience that demonstrates God's miraculous provision in response to the faithfulness of His children. A woman received a bill that was due by Monday of the following week and it was critical that it be paid. She had recently begun living by these principles, but she had no money at this time to pay the bill. She was very concerned. Our friend encouraged her to do everything she could and trust in God do the rest and supply her need. They prayed and asked God to supply the need. The day before the bill had to be paid the woman still did not have the money. While vacuuming her home, her vacuum cleaner bag burst and blew dust and dirt everywhere. As she was searching for a replacement bag to clean up the mess, she found thirteen $50 bills stacked on a shelf in a closet. They had not been there two days earlier. How did they get there? I guess only God knows, but the bill was paid on time. Through all of this the woman was not sitting idly, waiting for God to do something. She was doing everything that she knew to do, but the situation was out of her control.

This may sound extraordinary but many things like this have happened to those who put their trust in God. Consider this: **Sometimes we ignore things that God does in our life because we fail to recognize them.** If we are always seeking spectacular and miraculous occurrences we tend to miss many simple provisions and blessings. Let me illustrate.

A man slipped and was falling from a rooftop. He cried "God help me!" As he slid down the roof his belt snagged on a nail and stopped his fall. As he was climbing back up he said, "never mind God, I'm OK now." His cry was answered but he failed to recognize or acknowledge it.

Another story illustrates the same thing.

A flood came upon a small community and the waters began rising. A man of STRONG FAITH was standing on his porch observing the water that was about a foot deep. A large transport truck came along rescuing people and taking them to higher ground. This man declined the help and said that he was believing God to rescue him. The water rose to about eight feet deep and a boat came by to pick up the man who was now on the porch roof. He declined and responded as before. Finally, up to his waist in water while standing on the highest point of his house, a helicopter came to save him. He still refused and was confident that God would miraculously save him. He drowned. Upon arriving in heaven, obviously puzzeded and disappointed, he asked God, "why didn't you save me? I never doubted and I held on to the end." God replied, "I sent a truck, a boat and a helicopter, what more did you want?". This may be a funny little story but this attitude can be seen in some people. I believe in miracles and we have seen them,but I want to point out that many times miracles may come in the form of rescue boats or planes. The results are equally as great so don't miss a blessing by ignoring the obvious.

We have been discussing truth and faith operating together. When God has said something, it is true but that truth is not always evident in our lives. Faith can bring it into evidence.

Romans 4:17 (as it is written, "I have made you a father of many nations") in the presence of Him whom he believed; God, who gives life to the dead and calls those things which do not exist as though they did;

This verse says that God speaks of things that don't exist as though they did. This is an example of FAITH in action. God uses the same principles that He gave us to use. You can use faith in the same way that God uses it. If God's word says something about you, you can also say it because it is true. You can declare it even if it doesn't exist at the time. This principle is hard for us to grasp because it is beyond just our mind. It goes into the spirit. Remember, truth coupled with faith, brings into existence things that did not previously exist.

In our generation many people are interested in the spiritual realm. Truth that changes people's lives operates by the laws and principles of the spiritual realm. The spiritual is a higher order than the natural. It controls the natural. Truth, typically is not found through religion because religious people are usually trying to reach a spiritual goal by natural means. Truth is acquired by spiritual relationship with God. Spiritual experiences outside of a relationship with Jesus Christ, end up in error rather than truth.

Understanding that TRUTH originates in the spiritual realm will help in applying it in our lives. The laws of physics are fact and they do not change but when spiritual interacts with natural,, the laws of physics are often overruled. There are multitudes of examples of miracles in the bible. Things like Jesus walking on water or raising the dead. There are ocassions of water being turned into wine, feeding 5000 men with five loaves and two fish, and blind and lame people being instantly healed. As I have stated, this book is written from a christian perspective which assumes a literal belief in the truth and accuracy of the bible. Even so, there is other evidence of things that defy natural laws. Levitation, or the bending of metal objects by psychic power are examples of power beyond the natural. I include some of these things simply to show that christians are not the only people who believe in spiritual things, but from a biblical perspective they are the only ones who have the potential to know the truth.

Truth is absolute. It is always true regardless of what we think or feel. It is comforting to know the truth, we can bank on it. We can stake our lives on it. A word of caution: We look to the bible for truth but people sometimes arrive at something other than the truth. How can several people read the same text and believe such a diversity of things? If we stake our lives on something that we think is truth and it turns out not to be true, we could be in serious trouble.

Truth is consistent throughout the bible. This fact can be helpful in verifying whether someting is true or not. If you have discovered a truth, it will be in harmony with every other text in the bible that deals with the same topic. Sometimes things are not considered in their context and other times they are simply mis-understood. For example, we consist of spirit, soul and body. There are principles that apply to each of these areas. If someone tries to apply a soul principle to the spirit, it may not fit or apply. We must compare apples with apples so to speak. Truth builds upon truth in a way similar to mathematic principles building upon each other to form higher level equations. The simple laws of hermeneutics are helpful in determining the truth. They are as follows:

Hermeneutics: The science and art of Interpretation.

1. Consider the purpose of the bible as a whole.
2. Consider the distinct message of each book.
3. Know to whom the writing is addressed.
4. Understand the immediate context.
5. Compare other scripture that is related to the same topic.
6. Understand the words of the context. (Original language)
7. Avoid prejudice or pre-conception.

How can truth set us free? *By knowing it*! If it was true that we had $500,000.00 in our bank account and we knew it, we would think and act differently than if the balance was $5.00. If we had the money but didn't know it, our life wouldn't change. What we know, affects how we live, therefore we need to know what is true.

Chapter 7

KNOWLEDGE = POWER: Principle #4

Knowledge, (as we are using it) is more than intellectual awareness of something. It is being sure. It is knowing beyond any doubt.

There are many things that we do without understanding the underlying principles. Using lights or electric appliances is an example. Many of us know how to turn on a light switch or tune a radio to a station, but if the light fails to come on or the radio doesn't work, we might have to call someone to repair them. There may be some principles that we may never need to know but there are also basic principles that if they were known would make life much easier.

> **Life's problems like mathematical word problems, don't come to us in equation form. We must _find_ the equation to solve them**

Here is an example of the difference between simple awareness and practical working knowledge: When I was studying algebra I enjoyed word problems. A word problem is a problem that is written in story form with no given equation. For example: If you traveled 100 miles and your vehicle uses one gallon of fuel for every 20 miles you travel, how many gallons of fuel did you use? The answer is 5 gallons. If you didn't know or understand the principles you might have a difficult time solving the problem. If the problem was written like this: $100 \div 20 = ?$ it would be very simple to solve. Many people are familiar with some of *life's equations* but unless we know how and where to find them when we need them, we probably won't solve our problems. Even if we know where to find the answers, we need also to know how to apply them. Life's problems like word problems in math, don't come to us in equation form. We must find the equation to solve them. We need knowledge of the truth, along with faith to solve life's problems.

There are several examples that support the fact that knowledge brings power. The word "knowledge" in the following examples, is the Greek word "epignosis" which means; a clear and exact knowledge that powerfully influences the life of the one who "knows". This type of knowledge is more powerful and useful in our lives than simply being aware of something.

Ephesians 4:11-13 And He Himself gave some to be apostles, some prophets, some evangelists, and some pastors and teachers, {12} for the equipping of the saints for the work of ministry, for the edifying of the body of Christ, {13} till we all come to the unity of the faith and of the KNOWLEDGE of the Son of God, to a perfect man, to the measure of the stature of the fullness of Christ;

Notice here that a full knowledge of the Son of God moves us toward maturity and completeness. As we continue you will see that all of these principles work together in harmony with each other. They build upon each other. We have discussed Faith and Truth and now we are focusing on (KNOWING the Truth).

Hebrews 4:2   For indeed the gospel was preached to us as well as to them; but the word which they heard did not profit them, not being mixed with faith in those who heard it.

You can see here in Hebrews 4:2 that hearing the word of truth and even knowing the truth is not quite enough. Knowledge and truth must be combined with faith to bring results. Let's look at another example.

2 Peter 1:2-3   Grace and peace be multiplied to you in the KNOWLEDGE of God and of Jesus our Lord, {3} as His divine power has given to us all things that pertain to life and godliness, through the KNOWLEDGE of Him who called us by glory and virtue,

Grace, peace and all things that pertain to life and godliness come to us through the KNOWLEDGE of God. The next verse reveals that we can escape the pollutions of this world through the KNOWLEDGE of God.

2 Peter 2:20 For if, after they have escaped the pollutions of the world through the KNOWLEDGE of the Lord and Savior Jesus Christ, they are again entangled in them and overcome, the latter end is worse for them than the beginning.

In reviewing this principle you can see that by having a personal knowledge of God and His word, we have the ability to find the equations that will solve any of our problems. Knowing God gives us the ability to understand and know His word. 2 Peter 2:3 says that we have ALL THINGS that pertain to life, through the knowledge of Him. "All things" means; All Things, therefore it is important that we learn what our operating manual and warranty book (The Bible) says about life. The more we know, the more power we have at hand to change our lifes conditions.

Chapter 8

WHAT YOU SAY IS WHAT YOU GET:
Principle #5

This principle overlaps with others we have covered. It is similar to the first principle we discussed, "Thoughts Lead to Action". It involves our thinking, faith, knowledge and speech. This principle in operation can be observed in your environment. It is probable that when someone is suffering from stress, the underlying reason will be revealed in their conversation if you listen long enough. Let's look at a few scriptures and then illustrate it for clarifcation.

> # Believing causes an inward change, but speaking brings an outward change.

Romans 10:9-10   that if you [*confess with your mouth*] the Lord Jesus and [believe in your heart] that God has raised Him from the dead, you will be saved. {10} For with the heart one believes unto righteousness, and with the mouth confession is made unto salvation.

This is a very important principle. Notice that believing causes an inward change, but speaking brings an outward change.

Mark 11:23 "For assuredly, I say to you, whoever says to this mountain, 'Be removed and be cast into the sea,' and [*does not doubt in his heart*], but believes that those things he says will be done, [he will have whatever he says].

Here again, change in our tangible environment begins when we verbalize the true thoughts and desires of our heart.

Matthew 12:34-37 "Brood of vipers! How can you, being evil, speak good things? For [*out of the abundance of the heart the mouth speaks*]. {35} "A good man out of the good treasure of his heart brings forth good things, and an evil man out of the evil treasure brings forth evil things. {36} "But I say to you that for every idle word men may speak, they will give account of it in the day of judgment. {37} ["*For by your words you will be justified, and by your words you will be condemned.*"]

The words that we speak are very important. What we feed into our heart is very important because thats where our conversation originates, and our conversation changes our lives either for better or for worse. Our heart and mind are similar to computers. You have probably heard the statement; "Garbage in - Garbage out". If the words that we speak carry so much weight, we must become the master over them. Even in joking, people sometimes say things that have a devastating affect on the lives of others. There are many places in the bible that address the issue of guarding our tongue or being careful of what we say. We won't pursue them here but you can see that it's wise to think before we speak.

It is important to remember that we live and operate in three dimensions; spirit, soul and body. When we speak, there is an unseen dimension around us, observing and listening to what we say. Remember, the spiritual is a higher order than the natural and it influences what takes place in the natural. The things we speak have affect in all three dimensions even though we may not see it at the time. We talked about the power of the mind earlier. When the mind is in harmony with the spirit, our life becomes peaceful. When our spirit, soul and body are in harmony, inner conflict ceases and we are at rest.

Confession is a word that means different things to different people. In this context, confession simply means this; "the words that we speak and the things that we talk about". It does not mean telling our life's secrets or sins to someone. Another word for confession is speech. The word "believe", in the bible is the same greek word that is translated "faith". When our faith is developed by hearing and knowing the truth, our thinking changes and we talk differently. You might say that confession is the trigger of faith. We have already seen that faith changes things on the inside or in the spiritual realm, but confession brings it into reality where we can see it. Speaking is the end of the process that initiates the changes in our lives. God does what He does by speaking words. Example: God SAID, "let there be light".

Jesus said that our words originate in the heart. (Matt 12:34-37) If you think about it you will find that people talk about the things that are foremost in their hearts and minds. Have you ever seen a group of men or boys watching passing women and whistling or making comments? What do you suppose was in their heart? The thoughts in their heart are being expressed through their mouths. Some people love to talk about sports, some love to discuss the latest gossip. It is apparent that the things that motivate us or excite us the most are the things that are most dominant in our hearts. They are the things that we usually talk about.

Listen to this verse from Proverbs.

Proverbs 18:21 Death and life are in the [*power of the tongue*], And those who love it will eat its fruit.

> # We will usually act or react the same way every time in a situation, until *our program* is changed

The words that we speak are so powerful, they can destroy a person. How can we improve our conversation and make it constructive rather than destructive? The simple answer to that question is [to put something different into our heart.] The result will be different words coming out of our mouths. We will deal with this more in the next chapter about sowing and reaping. Our mind is similar to a computer. How a computer responds in any given situation is determined by it's program. We will usually act or react the same way every time in a situation, until *our program* is changed. This is very important to understand because most of the things we do and say are done without deliberate thought. We simply act or react automatically.

How can we apply this to overcome stress? We begin by believing that God has a solution to our situation. This is faith. Then we find the truth about our situation and meditate on it until it becomes real to us. The resulting knowledge, combined with faith, has the power to change things. The solution to our situation is now being established in our heart and confidence of victory is growing. The trigger for the victory is initiated by speaking it. Once we know the answer and it is established in our heart we must declare it. If a person had the winning number in a lottery, he would have the right to collect the money. Knowing you have the winning number gives you confidence that you can collect, but unless you SPEAK UP, the prize will go unclaimed and do you no good.

Chapter 9

WE REAP WHAT WE SOW: Principle #6

Galatians 6:7 Do not be deceived, God is not mocked; for whatever a man sows, that he will also reap.

This is a straight forward principle, yet it is often mis-understood. Sometimes we wonder; "why me Lord?," or "how did I get into this situation?". Most of the time we bring our circumstances upon ourselves by the things that we have said, done, or chosen.

Good and bad seed both produce fruit - Be careful what you sow

---

The principle of sowing and reaping can be used to bring a positive change to our lives. For example; if a person suffers from depression and loneliness, they could begin encouraging others and being friendly to those who have no friends. By sowing encouragement and friendship, encouragement and friendship will be reaped. Another way of stating this is: "what goes around comes around". Our attitudes are very important.

If we have a critical attitude toward others we can expect critical attitudes toward ourselves.

The Golden Rule makes a lot of sense when we think of it in terms of sowing and reaping. Whatever we want people to do to us, we should do to them. It could also be said that whatever we do to others, others will do to us. Spiritual truth is often illustrated by natural examples. Agriculture for example: When a seed is sown, it produces a crop (of it's own type). The crop is reaped *later than it is sown* (it takes time). The harvest is *more than what was sown* (multiplied return). This holds true in the spiritual realm also. If we sow hate, sooner or later we reap hate. If we sow love, we reap love.

The parable of the sower can be found in Luke 8:5-8. The interpretation for it is in verses 11-15. Let's look at one portion of it.

Luke 8:11 "Now the parable is this: [**The seed is the word of God**].

We have determined that God's word is TRUTH and that the knowledge and application of truth brings change. Here in the parable of the sower we see that God's word is also seed. There is another story about an enemy who planted bad seed along with the good that had already been planted. This parable of the good and bad seed shows that both will grow in the same envirement. Therefore we must be careful to speak (sow) good things rather than bad because both will produce their fruit.

You will find that for every area of life, the laws, answers, methods and means are found in God's word. It is our handbook for living, our *bag of seed* so to speak.

Six principles have been briefly explained. Now let's look at some more specific information and illustrations on how to use them as tools to fix life's problems.

Chapter 10

RHEMA
Speaking to the Heart!

I mentioned that if someone had the entire bible memorized but it was only in the head and not in the heart, it would be of little value to them. The word "rhema" was mentioned in the chapter on faith. Let's expand on it's meaning and usage.

Rhema, translated from greek to english means; "word". It has a more personal application than "logos", which is another greek word that is also translated "word" in english. Following is a simple explanation of the meaning and use of the words is as follows:

> ## Logos is <u>hearing about</u> God,
> ## Rhema is <u>hearing</u> God

Logos for our application, is the [written] word of God. It is general and widely applicable. Rhema on the other hand is generally the [spoken] word and is more personal and specific. Let me illustrate.

Have you ever read or even memorized something in the bible and later while reading it again or thinking about it, it came alive to you. Maybe something that you didn't understand suddenly became clear. It became **Rhema** to you. Here is another example: If you are reading the bible you are reading the "logos". If while you are reading, God speaks to you through the text, the logos then becomes "rhema". In a nutshell, Logos is <u>**hearing about**</u> God, Rhema is <u>**hearing God**</u>.

The thought of God communicating directly with us is foreign to many people. Among those who have a relationship with Him, it is normal. I mention this to point out that hearing about God or His word is not enough to change circumstances in our lives. Many well meaning people have tried to test God and His word (LOGOS) by academic application (from the head not from the heart). This kind of approach usually fails and discourages those who try it. It also promotes skepticism because we wonder why it didn't work. Following are two scenerios that I have observed among folks that I personally know.

Faith comes from hearing "Rhema"
not from hearing "Logos"

A person is sick and they have heard from James 5:14-15 that if they call for the elders and have them pray, they will be healed. There is some doubt whether this will work but they decide to test it out. So they call the elders and they pray and nothing happens. The conclusion is that the verse didn't really mean what it said or that it wasn't God's will to heal in this case. Neither of these conclusions is true. In situations like this, people read the logos and try to act on it without it being personal to them. The faith, (absolute believing in the heart) was not there. It was only an academic test, not something that they would stake their life on. It was believing in the head but not in the heart. Remember, faith comes from hearing "Rhema" not from hearing "Logos".

Let's look at the other side of the same coin. I have seen other people in the same situation. In their case the person who was sick was convinced in their heart that God had spoken to them (Rhema), and that He would heal them. The result? - They were healed.

When God speaks to us, and we hear and respond by faith, the promised result occurs *every time*, no exceptions. The point is that we need to learn to hear God's voice (rhema). When we hear it and act on it, things happen. These examples again point back to the difference between knowing in the head and knowing in the heart. Most people who are mature in faith have experienced both sides of this coin. Most people fell before learning to walk. It's a growing experience.

Healing is only one example that illustrates the importance of truly hearing God's voice. Let me say it another way. There may be things in your life that you know need to be changed. You can read about it clearly in the bible but for some reason you just never deal with it. When God Himself gets your attention and says "It's time to make that change", you would probably make the change. That's what "Rhema" is. It is when God gets through to us on an individual basis. It is an interaction that goes beyond the mind and into the heart.

As stated before, the cure is very simple. The application is the part that takes faith, knowledge, perseverance, and discipline. The following are four verses that bring clear the importance of truly HEARING God's voice on a continuing basis. The word Rhema is used in each of these verses:

Matthew 4:4 But He answered and said, "It is written, 'Man shall not live by bread alone, but by every WORD that proceeds from the mouth of God.' "

Man doesn't live only by natural food, but by hearing God.

John 15:7 "If you abide in Me, and My WORDS abide in you, you will ask what you desire, and it shall be done for you.

Jesus said that if His words (Rhema) lived in us, we could ask whatever we wanted and it would be done. This shows God's confidence in the people who really listen to and obey Him.

Romans 10:17 So then faith comes by hearing, and hearing by the WORD of God.

Faith is generated and grows by hearing God. Remember that we cannot even please God without faith.

Ephesians 6:17 And take the helmet of salvation, and the sword of the Spirit, which is the WORD of God;

We are told to take up the sword of the Spirit, it is the weapon that will defeat stress. It will only work if it is real in our hearts and not just information in our heads. God speaks His word to us, and we in turn speak it to our situation.

Before I begin summarizing the principles and their application, I want to share one other principle that affects everything that we do. It is a key in applying God's spiritual laws.

Chapter 11

Principle #7:
With God all things are possible, without Him we can do nothing.

We have discussed things that can bring peace, joy, and victory over stress. We often either forget or do not understand that we do not have the ability (by ourself) to do or apply these things in our lives. They are true and they work but the thing that makes them work is the POWER of God. We must tap into His power and ability.

Sometimes our efforts are what hinder us from pressing on through obstacles. Sometimes we get so involved in trying to climb out of a pit, that we fail to notice an elevator that is available. God did not design us to make it under our own power. He is the power that gets the job done. When we try to do His part we get tired and depressed and stressed because it's too big for us. Consider the following three scriptures.

God did not design us to make it on our own

John 15:5 "I am the vine, you are the branches. He who abides in Me, and I in him, bears much fruit; for [*without Me you can do nothing*].

Romans 7:18-19 For I know that in me (that is, in my flesh) nothing good dwells; for to will is present with me, but [*how to perform what is good I do not find*]. {19} For the good that I will to do, I do not do; but the evil I will not to do, that I practice.

1 Peter 5:6-7 Therefore humble yourselves under the mighty hand of God, that He may exalt you in due time, {7} [*casting all your care upon Him*], for He cares for you.

God did not design us to make it on our own. We need Him to live successfully. Without Him we can't do anything. We desire to do good but can't seem to do it consistently. He tells us to cast our care upon Him, it's to heavy for us to carry. The previous verses show that we can't solve our problems by our own efforts. The next few scriptures point out God's ability working in and through us:

Mark 10:27   But Jesus looked at them and said, "With men it is impossible, but not with God; for [*with God all things are possible*]."

Luke 18:27   But He said, "The things which are impossible with men are [*possible with God*]."

Matthew 11:28-30   "Come to Me, all you who labor and are heavy laden, and I will give you rest. {29} "Take My yoke upon you and learn from Me, for I am gentle and lowly in heart, and you will find rest for your souls. {30} "For [*My yoke is easy and My burden is light*]."

The emphasis of these passages is that NOTHING is impossible with God. Many things are difficult or impossible for us using our own ability. Something as simple as love, as described in 1 Corinthians, chapter 13, is impossible for man to do. This same love that is impossible for us, is natural for God.

Acts 1:8   "But [*you shall receive power*] when the Holy Spirit has come upon you; and you shall be witnesses to Me in Jerusalem, and in all Judea and Samaria, and to the end of the earth."

We have received power to initiate positive changes in our lives. That power is God working in us. Simply knowing that we don't have to make it by our ability should relieve some stress. We have a helper with real power working with us to defeat it. He is the Spirit of God.

The bible says in Philippians 4:13 that "I can do all things through Christ who strengthens me." I want to share an experience that demonstrates the power of God at work with His principles.

In 1972 a friend and I purchased a mobile home. We had looked at many models and finally found one we thought we liked and would fit into our budget. Together we paid $1000.00 as a down payment and closed the deal. When the home arrived at the park where we had rented a space, we went to look it over. The set-up was complete but the finishing work had not been done. There were loose pieces of molding and debris that needed to be cleaned up. Things didn't look quite the same as they did when we bought it. A feeling of depression and despair came over both of us. We were both convinced that we had been much too hasty in our decision. We were both 23 years old at the time and had spent all the money we had on this home and we now thought that we had made a big mistake. It was too late to reverse the deal. We had no cash reserves and now had a mortgage payment for a home we didn't want or even like. I was very depressed. I hated this new home and I was ready to pack up everything and move back to New Jersey where my family was. I was ready to leave the mobile home there and run away. My roommate felt the same way. He was from Ohio and he was ready to take off also. Our feelings were probably similar to those of a retired person who had just been conned out of his life savings. [Our feelings, as real as they were, were not based on fact or reality. They were based on our perception of a situation.] This is a good example of how the devil can drive us to depression or worse by simply influencing our thinking. Some of you may be able to relate to this. The circumstances may have been different but the effect was the same. We were stressed to say the least. We decided that eating might make us feel better so we went to a restaurant to get a bite to eat. As we were driving I was thinking (having a pity party) and suddenly something inside of me (it was the Spirit of God) said; "you should be thankful that you have a home, you should apologize to God for your lousy attitude. Be thankful and dedicate your home to Him." When we got our food we thanked God for it and apologized to Him for our attitudes. We thanked Him for our new home and asked Him to bless it. We apologized for not including Him more in the whole process and we asked Him to help us with our attitudes.

That was more than 20 years ago and I didn't know a lot of of the things that I do now but something happened that I will never forget. I was applying the principles that I have been sharing with you even though I wasn't fully aware it. The sequence was something like this:

** God spoke ** I heard Him ** I became aware that my thinking was out of order ** and ** I cried HELP **.

When we came back to the home about an hour later, we walked in and a miracle took place. Both my friend and I experienced a complete and instantaneous change of attitude. We suddenly liked the place. Let me describe this miracle. This attitude change was a very unusual occurrence. We went from an intense negative emotion, (really bummed out), to the opposite, (feeling real good), in an instant. Nothing had changed except our thoughts but the effect was like life or death. We were so grateful for our new home. We knelt down and dedicated the home to God. We were really happy and filled with the joy of being new home-owners. I haven't experienced such a total and instant change in my feelings and attitude before or since that event. This demonstrates the POWER of God and His principles working to give victory over stress and depression. Several of the best years of my life were during the time I lived in that home. I want to encourage you to trust God with your life and allow His power to get rid of the stress in your life. We truly can do all things through Christ who strengthens us.

Was this a once in a lifetime occurrence or does it work all the time? Let me share a recent experience.

I have been living by these principles for years now. I know God much better now than I did then, and I am also more familiar with His word. When I began this book I had the opportunity to be overwhelmed by stress. I overcame the pressure and maintained some level of peace by applying what I am writing. This is proof of the pudding so to speak.

As I mentioned at the beginning of this book, I was given notice near the end of October, 1991, that I was being laid off from the company that I had worked for since 1972. Contracts were ending and the work force was being reduced by nearly 2000 employees. Starting over at 42 years old was certainly not my dream but that was what I was facing. I think this qualifies for a potential stress situation. There were many others who terminated employment at the same time I did and I could see depression, bitterness and other signs of stress. I will share the steps that I took and the results I experienced. This book is a by-product of the experience.

I had been practicing these things for several years. I developed a lifestyle of monitoring my thoughts and feeding good things into my mind and heart. I took some time each day to read my bible. I had done this every day for nearly 8 years. The daily reading of God's word developed faith and put good things in my heart. My wife and I were faithful stewards of our finances. What all this means is that I had been trying to sow good things on a regular basis for some time. You may notice that I have been using words like **daily, lifestyle, continuous,** etc. It is very important that we understand that change is normally not instant, it takes time. The thing that makes it work is a daily, continuing effort and application of these principles. I used the example of the black belt martial artist. You can't become a black belt by going to a few lessons and then practicing for only a few weeks. It takes time and regular practice.

When I became unemployed I did not stop sowing, but continued to do the things that had done for years. The result was a confidence that God would see to it that I succeed and prosper. My life took some new directions, and desires that I had in my heart for years began coming to pass.

If you are encouraged by this book, one of my desires has been fulfilled. I received some instruction from God and was encouraged by Him. Because of this relationship with Him, I was able to overcome worry and depression. I was reaping what I had sown in previous years. Let me share some of the scriptures that helped me move toward that goal.

Two scriptures that I continually had in my mind were Joshua 1:8 and Psalm 1:1-3. Both of these are listed in the chapter on Thoughts leading to Action. They promise fruitfulness and prosperity to those who meditate on, and obey God's word. I fully expect continued fruitfulness and prosperity because I have been doing these things regularly. Because of an attitude of seeking God's kingdom, and a faithfulness in giving financially to God's work, I also expect to reap the promises concerning material needs.

Here are some scriptures I look to for material needs: Matthew 6:31-33, Philippians 4:19, Proverbs 3:9-10, and Malachi 3:10. They promise that our needs will be met and we will be blessed as a result of faithfulness to God and His word. A person in partnership with God - **cannot fail.**

There are many things involved in overcoming stress and they all work together. Two things that are very important to remember are:

1. We cannot make it without the power of God helping us. It is nice to know that we are not expected to make it alone.

2. We MUST develop a trust in God.

We may have all the answers but if we don't trust God with our life, knowing the answers won't get the job done. The path is not always easy. I won't tell you that I didn't or don't have stress in my life, but I can overcome it when it comes, and you can too.

Chapter 12

SUMMARY:

Let's review the principles and see how they relate to each other. They are not in order of priority. This is simply the order in which they were addressed. These principles are spiritual laws that always work when they are applied correctly. For example, an airplane flies when the laws of lift and thrust are applied. Gravity is still working but it is being overcome by the operation of other laws. Similar effect can be seen in our lives when combinations of spiritual laws work together to overcome the ones that are keeping us from getting off the ground.

Spiritual laws ALWAYS work when they are applied correctly

Here are the principles again:

1. Thoughts give birth to Action.

2. Faith precedes reality.

3. Truth supersedes natural fact.

4. Knowledge brings power.

5. What you say is what you get.

6. What you sow is what you reap.

7. God and you can do anything, you without God, can do nothing.

People sometimes get disillusioned because of lack of understanding and/or out of context applications of scripture. Usually spiritual laws work in combinations with each other, like thrust and lift work together to overcome gravity. As you learn how these principles work, it is a good idea to get wise counsel to help in the process. In the bible we often see the church, (God's family) compared to a human body. Each of us is representative of some part of that body. In order for a body to operate properly, all the parts must function together. By seeking the counsel of others, we can help each other. **A word of caution**; don't ask for wise counsel from someone who has failed in what you are trying to do. In other words, if you have a leaky faucet, don't call an electrician, call a plumber. Remember when we are fighting for victory, we don't need sympathy, we need truth.

> # When we are fighting for victory, we don't need sympathy, we need truth

Let's look at how some of these laws work together. THINKING (Principle #1), SPEAKING (Principle #5), and SOWING (Principle #6) are all related. The foremost things in our heart are the things that we usually **think** about. We usually **talk** about the things we are thinking about. The words we say are **seeds** that are being sown, and we reap what we sow.

If there is one thing that I want to communicate in this book, it is the importance of what we think. **Thinking is the beginning of the process that determines our course in life**. Our actions and reactions won't change until our thinking changes. Make it a point to take a regular inventory of what you think about. As we discipline our thinking, our conversation begins to change and we begin planting new kinds of seeds. The result: a changed lifestyle. Be honest with yourself when you evaluate your thoughts. We tend to try to justify the way we are and the way we think rather than change it. People often compare themselves with someone else. Comparing yourself with others will almost always result in hurt rather than help. If you compare yourself to someone with greater weakness than yours, you will justify yourself as being not so bad, and you will not improve. If you compare with someone stronger than yourself, you get frustrated and may give up. If you must compare, use Jesus as your model, realizing that He is the perfect model and we don't measure up to Him. This gives you a standard to measure your improvement by.

Three other laws that generally work together are; FAITH (#2), TRUTH (#3), and KNOWLEDGE (#4). Since knowing the **truth** makes us free, it is a key element. Remember, it supersedes our senses. We get **knowledge** of the truth from God and His word. As we hear God, and get knowledge of the truth, **faith** develops. Faith then initiates changes in our heart which changes our thinking which changes our talking, and so on. You see how all these things work together in kind of a chain reaction to bring about a result.

Bad attitude can spoil good seed

God's laws operating in our lives are similar to the laws of nature. There is a balance to life. Many people are concerned about saving our planet because they believe the ecological balance has been upset. Many people are trying to get their lives together because the balance for their lives has been upset. The law of sowing and reaping is one that we should become very familiar with. The other principles interact with it and vary the results to some degree, but we always reap what has been sown. You did not get where you are in life by accident or chance. You are reaping what you have been sowing. You may say, "I have been sowing good but I'm reaping bad". Remember, there are several things involved in the process. We may try to sow what appears to be good seed, in ground that has been poisoned by an attitude of un-forgiveness or bitterness. The seed may be good but the ground may be bad. Sometimes we are unaware of attitudes that have been nullifying what we try to do, like an airplane with a big weight tied to it. Nothing is wrong with the plane, it just has excess weight that doesn't belong there.

Here is a helpful tip for finding hidden things that are hindering us. Develop a daily bible reading plan and listen to christian teachers as often as possible. Why? Let's look at a scripture from Hebrews.

Hebrews 4:12-13 For the word of God is living and powerful, and sharper than any two-edged sword, piercing even to the division of soul and spirit, and of joints and marrow, and is a discerner of the thoughts and intents of the heart. {13} And there is no creature hidden from His sight, but all things are naked and open to the eyes of Him to whom we must give account.

You see, God's word can discern between our thoughts (mind), and the intents of our heart. *Things that are hidden to us are not hidden to God.* As we listen to His word, He will give us the insight to identify things that are hindering us. It may be something minor or it could be major. Don't run from the light that will expose your inner self. Let God expose it, then let Him put it back in order. This light of God, the TRUTH, often makes us uncomfortable, but we must seek it and face it in order to reach our destiny. Ask God for wisdom, He will give it to you.

James 1:5 If any of you lacks wisdom, let him ask of God, who gives to all liberally and without reproach, and it will be given to him.

Principle (#7) is applicable to everything that we do. In order to be successful in all areas of life, (spirit, soul, and body), we must have a relationship with God. Remember, Jesus said that without Him, we can do nothing. (John 15:5) He is the power that enables us to change for the better. Have you ever heard the phrase; "It's my way or the highway"? If you read your bible carefully you will find that this is God's attitude. Jesus said that He is **THE WAY**, there is no other way to God except through Him. That is why we must understand that the only way to overcome life's trials and have *lasting* victory, is to do it **His way**.

It is much easier to learn and apply the laws of God if you are around other people who are doing the same. I have heard people say, "I don't need church or bible studies, I can have a relationship with God on my own". This is true, but a person can't survive very long alone. The bible likens us to individual parts of a body, we need each other for nourishment and encouragement. Ephesians 4:16 teaches this.

Ephesians 4:16   from whom the whole body, joined and knit together by what every joint supplies, according to the effective working by which every part does its share, causes growth of the body for the edifying of itself in love.

Without the safety of the whole body we tend to drift slowly into dangerous waters. Let me illustrate. You may have heard that if you put a frog into a pot of boiling water, it will immediately jump out. That's logical. The unusual thing is that if you put the same frog in a pot of room temperature water, then very slowly heat the water to boiling, the frog will not jump out, but will cook to death. The change is so gradual that the frog is deceived. We too, can slowly get ourselves into a situation that eventually could destroy us. It happens so gradually and subtly, that we don't recognize the danger until it's too late.

Become familiar with these principles. Think about them often, and continually monitor your thoughts and words. Read your bible daily and ask God to speak to you through it. Ask Him to reveal anything that should be changed, then find and apply the truth that can bring the change.

This book probably sounds partial or biased toward christian people. The reason is this; The principles or laws of life that God has designed, operate in everyone's life, but His promise of good things are to those who obey Him. They are for His children. We become His children by what Jesus called being born again. It is a spiritual birth into a new dimension. The bible says it like this:

2 Corinthians 5:17 Therefore, if anyone is in Christ, he is a new creation; old things have passed away; behold, all things have become new.

When a person is born again, they receive a new nature. This new nature desires to obey and please God. This new spiritual being that is formed in us has the power to help us apply God's principles. Without this new nature we cannot fulfil God's plan for us, and we cannot effectively live a life of peace. This experience of being born again or becoming a christian is discussed more in the chapter on God's viewpoint of christianity. Following is a scripture and an example that illustrates the need for a new nature.

2 Peter 2:22   But it has happened to them according to the true proverb: "A dog returns to his own vomit," and, "a sow, having washed, to her wallowing in the mire."

Why do dogs and pigs do this? Because they are dogs and pigs. If you could change a pig into an eagle, it would no longer wallow in the mud, it would soar in the sky. Likewise, if we want to experience the happy, prosperous, peaceful life that God designed for us, we must have a new nature. This new nature is God's nature. We become like Him and we leave the old nature behind. It's like dying and coming back to life as a new person in the same body. Consider the following scriptures:

2 Peter 1:4 by which have been given to us exceedingly great and precious promises, that through these you may be *partakers of the divine nature,* having escaped the corruption that is in the world through lust.

1 Corinthians 6:17 But he who is joined to the Lord is *one spirit with Him.*

Colossians 3:9-10 Do not lie to one another, since you have *put off the old man* with his deeds, {10} and have *put on the new man* who is renewed in knowledge according to the image of Him who created him,

Romans 6:4 Therefore *we were buried with Him* through baptism into death, that just as Christ was raised from the dead by the glory of the Father, even so *we also should walk in newness of life.*

The preceding verses all point to a dying of our old way of life and the beginning of a new one. They also show that God has given us the opportunity to be a partaker of His own nature.

When a person undergoes this transformation he truly becomes a brand new person. This new person begins on the inside (spirit). When we begin to apply the principles we have been discussing, the change that happened on the inside, brings change on the outside. Most programs work from the outside. God's program works from the inside. In fact, the model for prayer that Jesus gave His disciples supports this fact. He said to pray like this; "Thy kingdom come, Thy will be done, in earth as it is in heaven." The bible tells us that the kingdom of God (also called the kingdom of heaven), is within us. Having God's will done in earth as it is in heaven is simply having the reality of the spiritual realm brought into manifestation in the natural realm. God begins on the inside and works His way out until we can see the results in our lives.

Ultimately, who and what we are will always be manifest in what we do. Consider the following examples:

There once was a scorpion on the side of a river. A turtle came by and the scorpion asked him to ride on his back across the river. The turtle said no, because he did not want to be stung by the scorpion. The scorpion reasoned with the turtle that he wouldn't sting him because if he did, he would also drown in the river. After much debate the turtle agreed to take the scorpion across. As they were swimming across, the scorpion stung the turtle on the head and they began to sink as the poison took affect. The turtle cried out, "why did you do that, now we will both die?". The scorpion replied, "I don't know, **I guess it's just my nature".**

You may take an old farm mule and groom it and alter it's appearance to look like a thoroughbred race horse, but it will never run like a race horse because inside it is still a farm mule. Can you see the point? If we desire a permanent change on the outside, we must first have a permanent change on the inside.

Let's review the six principles.

We acquire **KNOWLEDGE** of the **TRUTH**. This generates **FAITH** which affects our **THINKING**. The result is a change in our **WORDS** which are seed that we **SOW**. We reap what we have sown and hopefully we learn from our experience. This learning generates more knowledge and the cycle continues. The key, as I said before, is *what we think.* Therefore we must be diligent to feed the truth into our minds.

Chapter 13

A 12 Step Method

The following is a list of twelve steps that many people have used to overcome various conditions in their lives. This type of program is widely used for those who desire to overcome a variety of addictions. One thing I want to point out, is that God, or a higher power, is not specifically defined in these steps. Each person defines their own god.

1. One must admit that he is powerless over his situation and his life has become unmanageable.

2. One must come to believe that a power greater than one self, can restore him to sanity.

3. Make a decision to turn your will and your life over to the care of God, as you understand Him.

4. Make a searching and fearless moral inventory of yourself.

5. Admit to God, yourself, and another person, the exact nature of your wrongs.

6. Be entirely ready to have God remove all these defects of character.

7. Humbly ask Him to remove your shortcomings.

8. Make a list of all people you have harmed, and become willing to make amends to them.

9. Make direct amends to these people wherever possible, except when it would injure them or others.

10. Continue to take personal inventory and when you are wrong, promptly admit it.

11. Seek through prayer and meditation, to improve your conscious contact with God as you understand Him, praying only for knowledge of His will for you, and the power to carry it out.

12. Having a spiritual awakening as a result of these steps, try to carry this message to others with similar problems and practice these principles in all your affairs.

These twelve steps have been used in various applications and forms, to successfully bring positive change in peoples lives. Unless the Higher Power is the God who created us, the results are limited. Programs of this type deal mainly with our soul and body. Apart from Jesus Christ, the only true God, no program can bring the permanent spiritual change that is necessary. The following is a true story of a personal friend of mine. It shows the operation of many of the things we have discussed.

A Changed Man

A friend of mine was involved in a program to help him recover from several addictions, one of which was alcoholism. He was doing very well in his program and his family was coming back together as a functional unit. Even though this man was not drinking or using drugs, he still had the disease/addiction. He attended regular support meetings where there were others who had similar problems. His wife worried that if he didn't continue to attend these meetings, their life would fall apart again. At this point his was a success story. His family was back together and he was keeping himself straight, but then something happened.

One of the men who was in his group shared a bible verse with him. The verse was 2 Corinthians 5:17 which we read earlier. It says that if any person is in Christ, he is a new creation, the old things have passed away. When my friend read this verse, God gave him a personal revelation from it. You see this man had recently become a born again christian. When he read this verse, God revealed to him that he was a new person. He used to be an alcoholic, but now that old person had passed away and the new person was not an alcoholic.

Remember the principles that we shared. Here's what happened: he found the truth about himself; he was a new creature. Once he knew this, it developed faith because God had spoken it to him. Then he believed it and began to talk about it. The result was and is that he is no longer an alcoholic, God completely delivered him from that condition. He never attended another meeting of that group, and today he and his whole family are happy and healthy, spiritually, emotionally and physically.

The reason I shared this story is not to minimize the effectiveness of programs like the one he was involved in. It is to show the contrast and difference between an ongoing struggle to overcome something, and a complete deliverance from it. If we live by the principles of Jesus Christ, we are not in a constant struggle to maintain peace. He said that His yoke is easy and His burden is light. (Matt 11:30) There is a great deal of hope for people who will apply these principles even if they don't personally know Jesus, but the only way to complete liberty and fulfillment is through Him.

I said before that God is quite narrow minded. Jesus said that there is NO way to God except through Him. He is THE way. This narrows the options for complete satisfaction in life to one, His way or no way. This is one of the main reasons that I am writing, to point to that narrow way that leads to life and liberty.

John 14:6   Jesus said to him, "I am the way, the truth, and the life. No one comes to the Father except through Me.

Chapter 14

EXAMPLE:

When I completed the first draft of this book I had been unemployed for only a few months. There was plenty of uncertainty about the future and lots of people willing to give advice and be pessimistic. Let's review the process of how stress attacks us and then I'll finish my story.

One thing that we have to recognize and fight against is the naturally negative environment that we live in. The thing or situation that causes stress, we will define as the *STRESSOR*. We respond in some way to the stressor. This is the *REACTION*. To successfully overcome the stressor we must know and act on the truth, we must do something. This is the *ACTION*.

The sequence of stress is:
STRESS → REACTION → ACTION

For example the STRESSOR comes and tells you that you are a failure. It says that someone else will succeed but you will not. In my case the stressor was saying to my mind; "In this economy you will never find a job with good benefits that pays like the one you had. You will not be able to provide comfortably for your family." "It's too late in life to start over, etc."

The REACTION is usually some form of agreement with the stressor. We may think, "yes that's probably true, or, I should have done things differently than I did". **We tend to view difficult situations as the end rather than *a beginning*.** We may think it's not even worth trying.

Many people go as far as thinking of suicide when depression begins to close in around them. When we are feeling down or defeated there are always people who will agree with us and help us keep on feeling bad. Stay away from people who will encourage your negative REACTION.

The ACTION is where we need the truth. We need people to encourage us, not add fuel to discouragement. We don't need to hear how hopeless life is. Find a winner to talk to, and stay away from the losers.

My wife and I tried to keep ourselves surrounded by positive people who would encourage us. Misery loves company. Have you heard that? If you talk to other people who are stressed out and are not overcoming it, they will probably promote a pity party. They will probably even join the party.

When you participate, your **focus** turns to the problem, the pain, the hopelessness, and not to hope and the solution. I already mentioned some of the scriptures that I clung to during this time of stress. Matthew 6:24-34 says that if we seek God's kingdom first, all the things that folks need and worry about will be taken care of by God. Romans 8:28 tells us that ALL things work together for good to those who love God and are called by Him. We also read in Proverbs 3:5-10 that if we will trust in the Lord with all our heart and not rely on our own understanding and insight, He will direct our paths. Also if we honor God with our possessions, He will prosper us.

These things are truth from God's word that bring comfort. The first step is to completely trust God's word. The STRESSOR will come and say; "you have heard all these things before but look at your situation, it's not going to work for you." The REACTION might be; "yeah that's probably right, it seems that this works for others but this looks hopeless for me." The ACTION must be a trust in the truth (Faith), regardless of what you feel or think. This comes by meditating on the truth and asking God to make it real to you. Continue until it becomes real to you.

The action is a result of faith, or a lack of it. I mentioned earlier that in bible language, (faith and believing) are the same. What you believe determines what you will have and experience. Remember the example of the placebos? Step two of the twelve step method is believing that a power greater than yourself can help you. Principles two and five that we shared with you both relate to believing with your heart. The reason this is so important is; if you don't believe that you can get out of the condition you are in, you won't. I said that action is a result of faith or lack of it. Lack of faith is simply fear. It is believing that you can't do what you want to do. We all believe something, the key is to believe the truth.

Begin *visualizing* yourself with your needs all met. Visualization is a term that means different things to different people. I am describing the **application** of the process that has been presented throughout this book. Remember that faith is the substance of things HOPED for. Hope is the situation that you are visualizing. It is the picture that you have in your heart and mind. The visualization process is an important one. If you don't have a clear image of your goal in your mind, you probably won't get as far as you want to. As you study God's word to learn your purpose and destiny, ask Him to reveal it to you. As God develops the vision, you can begin laying plans for fulfilling it. The bible says that without vision, the people perish. (Prov 29:18 KJV) **A word of**

caution: Your hope or vision must be based on the word of God, not your own ideas. It works like this:

You begin visualizing yourself having a career that will provide for your family, (God promised to provide for us and our families). As you focus on this goal, (the physical manifestation of a spiritual truth), you begin to move toward it. Priorities must then be set and followed. Remember, Jesus said that you cannot serve two masters. In the Ten Commandments God said that you shall have no other gods before Him. (Ex 20:3) This means that nothing in your life can have a higher priority than God or His plan for you. When we lose this focus, the principles don't seem to work like we want them to. Then stick with it until you reach your goal.

Patience is a very important factor reaching our goals. Patience does not mean gritting your teeth and enduring something. It is knowing that things are at work in God's timetable, and being willing to submit yourself to it.

James 1:2-4   My brethren, count it all joy when you fall into various trials, {3} knowing that the testing of your faith produces patience. {4} But let patience have <its> perfect work, that you may be perfect and complete, lacking nothing.

The end result of faith and patience is that you will not lack anything that you need.

Don't expect things on your timetable - God's plan is always better

My wife and I knew the truth concerning our situation and through prayer, meditating on God's word and surrounding ourselves with other encouraging believers, we became convinced of it. Then we began to plan. We had to determine the proper priorities and begin setting a course toward our goal. Timing is usually frustrating for most people. Don't expect things to happen on your timetable because God almost always has a better plan. Seek His direction in your planning. In the process of moving toward your goal, keep thinking and meditating on scriptures like Philippians 4:6-8. We have a promise of peace that transcends understanding.

We had to spend time listening for ideas from God. If you are in a similar situation, He may have a job in mind for you, or He may give you a idea for your own business. Don't limit your thinking, every successful person began somewhere.

How did it all turn out? It has been more than three years since I lost my job. I was unemployed for about a year. During that year I finished the first draft of this book, served as associate pastor of a small church in Tucson, Arizona and became licenced as a financial planner. I later became re-employed by the same company where I worked for 19 years. I am using the experience and training that I have acquired over the years to develop a ministry of helping and encouraging people in areas of stress, finance and spiritual maturity. For a period of several months neither my wife or myself were employed but the truth of God's word manifested itself through it all. Our financial obligations were always met and we didn't have to sell anything or move from our home. All of our debts have now been paid (except the mortgage) and we are diversifying our income sources. The principles in this book do work. They are not any easier for me to apply than they are for you. I encourage you to trust God with you present situation as well as your future.

Pressure is necessary for growth. We are always on life's journey and though there are times of rest, we will always face potential stress. Therefore we must learn to deal with it effectively because it will always be there.

I hope this has been helpful in communicating some answers to life's problems. The principles are very simple, yet they are often very difficult to live by. I want to mention once again the importance of carefully selecting the people that you spend your time with. The bible describes the church as a body. The cells in a body are greatly affected by the surrounding cells. If you are stressed out, don't spend your time around others who are stressed out, find people who have found out how to live in peace and spend time with them. If you are sick and want to be healed, don't go to someone who doesn't believe that God wants you well. Find someone who has been healed and believes that God will heal you.

Problem solving does not have to be a difficult thing.

1. Honestly identify the problem and evaluate it.
2. Find the truth or promise that relates to it.
3. Meditate on the truth until the knowledge of it produces faith.
4. Think about it, speak it, then do it.

ALL things are possible with God.

Chapter 15
Forgiveness

While reviewing things that I had been studying, it occurred to me that I had forgotten to include a very important ingredient for a peaceful life; FORGIVENESS. Forgiveness is more of a practice than it is principle, but it is an important one.

Jesus gave His disciples an instructive model for praying. It is what many have come to know as the Lord's Prayer. Following are a few lines from that model.

Mat 6:12 And forgive us our debts, *As we forgive* our debtors.

Mat 6:14-15 "For if you forgive men their trespasses, your heavenly Father will also forgive you. 15 "But *if you do not forgive* men their trespasses, *neither will your Father forgive your trespasses.*

The bible makes it clear that to experience a healthy relationship with God and with others we must practice forgiveness. We read in Mark 11:25 that if we have ANYTHING against ANYONE, we should forgive. A biblical meaning of the word forgive is; to (*lay aside, leave, let alone, let be, let go, put or send away, forgive*).

Mark 11:25 "And whenever you stand praying, if you have anything against anyone, forgive him, that your Father in heaven may also forgive you your trespasses.

We could then paraphrase this verse to read like this: Whenever you are coming to talk to God, if you have anything against anyone, let it go, send it away from yourself, forgive it, so that your heavenly Father can send away, lay aside and forgive anything that keeps you from receiving blessing from Him.

Since peace and joy come from God, unforgiveness can hinder us from having them in our lives. Unforgiveness enhances stress rather than diminishing it.

Forgiveness... sets the forgiver free

Unforgiveness causes bitterness (an emotional ailment), and it can cause physical ailments as well. Try this exercise. Close your eyes for a moment and think of someone who has hurt you in some way. It may have been physical or emotional. It may be someone who has cheated you, stolen from you, betrayed you or simply irritates you. As you think of these people and situations, how does it make you feel. Do you feel peaceful and full of joy? If you are like most people you are feeling angry or bitter and maybe would even like to see some revenge on these people. You can see the effect of not letting these things go and sending them away from you and your thoughts. Forgiveness sets the forgiver free. It is therapy for the forgiver more than it is a benefit for the forgiven. If you did this exercise and thought of someone who has done wrong to you, forgive them now.

How can we forgive someone who is not even sorry for what they have done or caused in our lives? Like many other things we have discussed in this book, forgiveness is more spiritual than physical or emotional. Forgiveness is similar to true love in the sense that it is a decision rather than a feeling. It also is true that we cannot forgive in the purist sense of the word, unless we have some help from God. Remember my illustration of how the attitudes of my room mate and myself were changed after asking God's help when we bought the mobile home? There is very little that we can permanently change in our lives without the help of our creator/designer.

This brings me to another story that illustrates the effect of forgiveness.   My room mate that I mentioned earlier, left Tucson to attend college in another state. During the course of the four years at college he developed the practice of thinking and acting more from his head than from his heart. He had several painful experiences and experienced rejection from some people that he loved. His combined experiences caused him to become bitter and resentful toward certain people. He gradually lost the joyful carefree attitude that he once had. The interesting thing is that he didn't realize what had slowly happened to him. One day while reading a book he came to a section that taught about forgiveness.   The proverbial light came on in his mind and he became aware of several people whom he had become bitter toward. Now accutely aware of the effects of this attitude, he went immediately to God and acknowledged his unforgiveness and made a choice to forgive those who had hurt him. Even though none of the people involved knew what he had done, his life was instantly changed. The joy and zest for life that had been slowly drained from him returned at once because he forgave.

If you are stressed by people and relationships that stir up bitterness and resentfulness, let them go. Forgive and be released from the ill effects of them. Remember, we are not really capable of forgiving in our own strength, so make the decision to forgive and ask God to help you frogive. Then sit back and enjoy the freedom that comes when people and situations can no longer steal your joy.

Chapter 16
Praise & Worship

What is praise? What is worship? This section also focuses more on practice than principle. Let's begin with **praise**.

In biblical context, praise means several things including: celebration, laudation, extending ones hands in praise or adoration, or to rave. The dictionary defines praise as commendation, expressing approval, applause, expressing adoration or glorifying.

> # Would you be depressed as you cheered for your favorite team when they made a touchdown?

As you consider the meaning of praise, notice that it's effect is to take one's mind off of self and focus on someone or something else. Have you ever watched a sporting event where a team or individual performed unusually well? Maybe someone made a score or a great play. Try to imagine being sad, depressed and burdened with stress while cheering for the team that made the play. As you can see, praise can be a temporary relief from stress and the worries of our environment.

Let's look at another application of praise and it's affect on our lives. The following verse says that God inhabits the praises of Israel. Studying the bible shows that God not only inhabited the praises of Israel, but He also inhabits the praises of His people of all generations. The word inhabit means; to dwell. This means that when we praise God, He stays near to us.

Psa 22:3 (KJV) But thou art holy, O thou that inhabitest the praises of Israel.

What benefits can we realize from being around God?

Psa 16:11 (KJV) Thou wilt show me the path of life: in thy presence is fulness of joy; at thy right hand there are pleasures for evermore.

This is exciting for me because I enjoy having fun and being around others who are full of joy. Psalm 16:11 may give you a different perspective on God as we analyze it. The word joy as used in this verse means; *blithesomeness or glee, gladness, joy, mirth, pleasure, rejoicing*. One of the dictionary definitions of mirth is **jocularity**, which is one of my favorite words. It sounds like being in the presence of God is fun. I don't want to make light of God's awesomeness but at the same time I want you to see that being around God is not a boring or tedious religious experience. The word "pleasures" in the same verse means pleasant or delightful. So what does this have to do with us?

As we begin to praise God in the midst of our (positive or negative) life's experiences, He comes on the scene in a way that brings joy and pleasure like we can't find or experience elsewhere. The more we practice a lifestyle of praise toward God, the more pleasant and full of joy our lives will become. It has been my experience that spending even a few quality minutes with God is much better than hours or days with anyone or anything else. Imagine what your experience would be if you included God in all of your relationships.

Why praise or worship God? For one thing, He is worthy of it. Look around at His creation. He has made a wonderful world for us to inhabit. There are many things to praise Him and be thankful for. How about the air you breath?

What is worship? Worship simply means to bow down or to prostrate oneself in reverence and homage. When one comes into the presence of God through praise the result is a worship experience. As we encounter God's manifest presence it is so overwhelming that we cannot help but worship Him.

It is more difficult to relate the experience and practice of worship to the routine experiences of life. We may often praise someone or something but it would be quite unlikely that we would bow ourselves down before someone or something. The point is that when we are experiencing the act of worship, our mind is totally focused outward rather than inward. Our problems and stress melt away and for a time, become non-existent.

Praise and Worship of God should be a normal lifestyle for a child of God, although it often isn't. It would be worthwhile to frequently remind ourselves to stop and take time to praise the Lord. The practice of Praise and Worship recharges our batteries so to speak. It gives us the opportunity to experience the healing and joy that come from the awesome presence of God our creator.

Chapter 17

THE BODY

Up to this point we have dealt with the spirit and soul of man. These are the areas that I wanted to focus on, but our physical body is also an important factor in our lives. I am not a doctor or nutritionist so I will not try to give advice in those areas but I do want to point out some commonly known things about our bodies. We seem to be in a generation of physical fitness and we hear a great deal about nutrition. It is commonly known that the things we eat have a significant affect on the function of our body. It is also generally known that the chemical balance and physical condition of our body can greatly affect our emotions. Women who have experienced menopause would probably confirm this statement. The point it this: stress and emotional upset can also be caused by deficiencies or imbalances in our bodies. One of the best ways to bring our body into subjection, is through FASTING. You may be amazed at the simplicity and the affect of fasting. Fasting coupled with prayer can help in identifying the root cause of your stress. Consult your doctor before attempting to fast.

Occasional fasting, physical exercise, and proper nutrition can be of great help in reducing stress. I recommend that you find a good book on fasting, one on nutrition and one on exercise and make the appropriate changes in your diet and physical activity. It is sad to say but many of the "goodies" that we eat do more harm to our lives than good. The care of our bodies is a little different than the care of our soul and spirit but there are also many similarities. We need to find the **truth** and then diligently follow it. Discipline is very important in every area of our lives. Search your bible for examples of nutrition and fitness. One such example can be found in Daniel 1:5-16.

Let's move back into the spiritual arena now. The last section of this book is a brief description of God's view of christianity. I have used the term "Born Again Christians" and have said that christianity and religion are two entirely different things. I want to encourage anyone who does not have a personal relationship with Jesus Christ, to begin one right now.

THOUGHT: If you have been learning and applying God's principles in your life, it can be very encouraging to look back a few years and see your progress. Think of the growth you have experienced and the victories you have won. These past experiences will help to build your faith for the present circumstances.

Appendix A

CHRISTIANITY FROM GOD'S VIEWPOINT

Following is an explanation of the gift that God has given to mankind. This book has been written from a christian perspective. Let's define the term christian. Many people associate christianity with religion but there is a difference.

There are many religions in our world today. There are many religious people in our world but they are not necessarily christian. In fact many religions are anti-christian. Being religious simply means to be disciplined or devoted to something or someone. A person could be religiously evil. I realize that christianity is a religion in a technical sense but because of the broad use of the term I want to make a distinction between the two.

My definition of religion is this: An attempt by man to be acceptable to or find favor with his god. Usually it involves rules or regulations, rituals and activities that gain the participant a greater acceptance with his god. There are many who claim to be christians who fit this description. The key in this definition is [Man's Performance], which can also be referred to as works.

If anyone other than God gets credit for any part of it....It's not true Christianity

Christianity on the other hand, is: A personal relationship as a son or daughter with the God who created heaven and earth and everything in it. This relationship is a gift that cannot be acquired by performance. It is a birthright and one can only possess it by being born into it, hence the term born again.

Religion is man attempting to climb up to God, true christianity is God transforming us and raising us to His level. This transformation and elevation is a gift from God. We cannot earn it or attain it by our efforts.

Following is a brief overview of some things that God has done and some scriptures that illustrate it.

When God created man, He gave him dominion over all of His creation. Adam made a bad choice and he violated God's command and was condemned as a result. God loved Adam and He made a provision for him to be forgiven but he was not restored to his former position at this time. One of the results of Adam's sin, was that all of his descendants were separated from God, just as he had been. This includes us. God loves all of His creation so He provided a way for us to be restored to His family and be forgiven for our sin which resulted from the nature that we inherited from Adam.

Remember the illustration of having a winning lottery or door prize ticket. As you consider the following scriptures, notice this: God has already assigned a ticket in your name, a birthright into His family. You will see that all you have to do is cash it in and receive this new life. To receive it simply believe it and speak it.

Romans 6:23   For the [wages of sin] is death, but the [gift of God] is eternal life in Christ Jesus our Lord.

Romans 3:23   for [all have sinned] and fall short of the glory of God,

John 3:16   "For God so loved the world that He gave His only begotten Son, that whoever believes in Him should not perish [but have everlasting life].

Romans 10:9-10   that if you [confess with your mouth] the Lord Jesus and [believe in your heart] that God has raised Him from the dead, you will be saved. {10} For with the heart one believes unto righteousness, and with the mouth confession is made unto salvation.

The bible says that the wages or consequence of sin is death. This is a spiritual death and separation from God. It goes on to say that the GIFT of God is eternal life. We also read that everyone has sinned, no exceptions. This means that we all have a death sentence. The good news is that because God loves us, He gave His Son to die in our place, thereby removing the death sentence. The work has been done, the gift of life is ours, we can become sons of God (see John 1:12). We must simply believe it and confess it with our mouth.

This sounds so simple. It is simple. Religion is complex and confusing but God's plan is very simple. It is difficult for us to accept because it doesn't require anything from us except to simply believe and receive it. Because God has designed it this way, He is the ONLY one who gets any credit for it. We can't point to ourselves and say; "see how good I am". We didn't deserve it and couldn't earn it, so we can take no credit for it. In God's economy there is no inequality of personal worth, we are all the same regardless of our past performance or status. The following scripture says it very nicely:

Ephesians 2:8-9 For by grace you have been saved through faith, and that not of yourselves; it is the gift of God, {9} not of works, lest anyone should boast.

God even gives us the faith to believe. I hope this has helped in explaining what christianity is and how we can be partakers of it. Jesus said that one must be born again (see John 3:3-7). This is what happens: When a person believes that God has given him life and he professes it saying, "God I receive it", God breathes spiritual life into that person and he/she is born again (from above) into God's family. This is where relationship comes in, we become His children. As God's children, we can now take advantage of all the promises and principles that He gave to His children in the bible.

Closing Words

The principles and information that have been shared in this book have proven themselves in the lives of many people. Let me emphasize once again the necessity of obedience to God's word. We can know the truth, we can believe it and talk about it. We can think about it and be thankful for it, but if we do not DO IT, it is of no benefit to us.

A man in Korea who pastors a church of over 500,000 people was asked what the secret of his success was. His reply was; "I pray, and I obey." Jesus said that His yoke is easy and His burden light. It is not a difficult thing to obey God's word, but we do have to yoke ourselves up with Jesus and DO IT. He, Jesus, likened those who hear and do His word, to wise people. Those who hear and don't do, are compared to foolish people.

James writes about doing Gods word:

- **James 1:22**   But be doers of the word, and not hearers only, deceiving yourselves.

- **James 2:17**   Thus also faith by itself, if it does not have works, is dead.

- **James 2:20**   But do you want to know, O foolish man, that faith without works is dead?

- **James 2:26**   For as the body without the spirit is dead, so faith without works is dead also.

We may say that we believe, but if there is no resulting action, our belief is useless. Remember the illustration about the wheelbarrow on the tight rope. Unless we are willing to get into the wheelbarrow, we don't have faith. Without faith it is impossible to please God. Jesus and His disciples frequently taught the importance of doing God's commandments.

The bottom line is this: You have information in this book and especially in your bible that will enable you to live in peace, joy and liberty from stress. Unless you DO IT on a continuing basis, it will be of no value to you.

You might say that the key to success in life is a few simple little words:

Find the TRUTH, Then <u>DO IT</u>.